THE REAL OF NATALIA GRACE

CALISTA MOON

All rights reserved. No part of this book may be reproduced, distributed, or transmitted in any form or by any means, including photocopying, recording, or other electronic or mechanical methods, without the prior written permission of the copyright owner except in the case of brief quotations embodied in critical reviews and certain other noncommercial uses permitted by copyright.

Copyright © 2025 by Calista Moon

Table of Contents

Introduction... 5

Chapter 1: The Adoption...................... 12

Chapter 2: The Mystery Unfolds.......... 21

Chapter 3: A House Divided................ 30

Chapter 4: Legal Battles and Public Scrutiny.. 38

Chapter 5: The Fight for Identity.........46

Chapter 6: The Fallout and Where They Are Now... 54

Conclusion..60

Introduction

The story of a seemingly innocent adoption spiraling into a shocking legal battle and media frenzy is one that has gripped the public for years. What started as a heartfelt attempt to provide a home for a child in need soon became a complex mystery filled with accusations, deception, and uncertainty. At the center of this controversy was a young girl, Natalia Grace, whose real age and identity were disputed by her adoptive parents. The case divided public opinion, with some seeing Natalia as a vulnerable child abandoned by those who swore to care for her, while others believed she was a manipulative adult who had conned her way into an unsuspecting household.

The bizarre nature of the case, filled with conflicting medical assessments, psychological evaluations, and legal rulings, made it one of the most controversial adoption stories in history. It raised difficult questions about trust, parental responsibility, and the role of the justice system in verifying identity. At its core, this was a deeply personal and painful ordeal for everyone involved.

As this book explores the various elements of the story, readers will be encouraged to question the narratives presented and form their own conclusions. Was Natalia a victim of neglect and misunderstanding, or was she a dangerous fraud? Were the adoptive parents misled, or were they complicit in a greater injustice? By analyzing the facts, testimonies, and media coverage surrounding the case, we will unravel the complex truth hidden beneath layers of speculation.

Ultimately, this is more than just a legal battle—it is a story about human nature, fear, and the consequences of doubt. The following chapters will delve into the key moments that shaped this case, the shifting perceptions of truth, and the lasting impact on those involved.

The Enigma of a Family's Nightmare

For the Barnett family, adopting Natalia Grace was supposed to be an act of love and generosity. Kristine and Michael Barnett believed they were giving a home to a vulnerable child with a rare form of dwarfism, spondyloepiphyseal dysplasia congenita. However, what began as a hopeful new chapter quickly turned into a nightmare, as suspicions arose about Natalia's true age and intentions.

From the start, inconsistencies in Natalia's behavior and physical development raised red flags for the Barnetts. They claimed that despite her small stature, she exhibited traits that seemed far beyond her supposed age. Reports of Natalia having a menstrual cycle, adult-like social interactions, and an advanced vocabulary led them to question whether she was really a child at all. This uncertainty escalated into fear as the Barnetts alleged that

Natalia displayed violent tendencies, including threats against the family's safety.

The confusion surrounding Natalia's identity fueled a spiral of paranoia and mistrust. The Barnetts sought medical opinions, some of which supported their belief that Natalia was older than she claimed, while others refuted it. In a controversial legal decision, a judge changed Natalia's birth records to classify her as an adult, further complicating the case.

What makes this ordeal particularly unsettling is the lack of definitive proof. Was Natalia a dangerous impostor who manipulated her way into the Barnett household, or was she an innocent child caught in the crossfire of a tragic misunderstanding? The case became an unsolvable puzzle, with every new revelation raising more questions than answers.

For the Barnetts, their act of kindness led to devastating consequences. The adoption that was meant to unite their family instead tore it apart, leaving behind a story filled with doubt, fear, and irreversible decisions.

The Intersection of Truth, Deception, and Media Frenzy

When the story of Natalia Grace and the Barnett family broke into mainstream media, it quickly became a sensationalized spectacle. The bizarre nature of the case—an adopted child possibly being an adult impostor—was irresistible to news outlets, talk shows, and documentary filmmakers. The public was captivated, drawn into a whirlwind of conflicting narratives, legal battles, and emotional testimonies.

Sensational headlines painted Natalia as either a villainous con artist or a helpless victim, while her adoptive parents were cast as either cruel abusers or terrified parents caught in an impossible situation. The lack of definitive answers only fueled speculation, with media platforms capitalizing on the uncertainty. Interviews, opinion pieces, and social media discussions turned the case into a public trial, where everyone had an opinion but few had the full truth.

The case was further complicated by previous media portrayals of similar scenarios. The film *Orphan* had introduced audiences to the fictional concept of a woman disguising herself as a child to infiltrate a family, and many drew comparisons between the movie and Natalia's story. While the similarities were purely coincidental, they shaped public perception and heightened skepticism about Natalia's claims.

True crime documentaries, including *The Curious Case of Natalia Grace*, sought to analyze the case in-depth, but they, too, were shaped by biases and selective storytelling. Every retelling of the case introduced new angles, making it difficult to separate fact from fiction. The media's influence on the case had real-world consequences, affecting the legal proceedings and the lives of everyone involved.

In the end, the case of Natalia Grace became more than just a family's private crisis—it became a cultural phenomenon, illustrating how the media can shape, distort, and amplify narratives until the truth becomes nearly impossible to discern.

Chapter 1: The Adoption

Adoption is often seen as an act of love and compassion, a way to provide a home for a child in need. For Kristine and Michael Barnett, adopting Natalia Grace was meant to be exactly that. In 2010, the couple welcomed Natalia into their Indiana home, believing they were adopting a six-year-old girl from Ukraine who had a rare form of dwarfism, spondyloepiphyseal dysplasia congenita. This condition affected her growth and mobility, making it appear even more urgent that she receive care and stability.

According to the Barnetts, Natalia's adoption was arranged quickly, without extensive background checks or thorough medical evaluations. Unlike a typical international adoption, which can take years, theirs was finalized in just a few months. They later expressed concerns that there was little documentation verifying Natalia's true age or history. Some adoption agencies rely on limited medical records and birth certificates from foreign countries, which are sometimes inaccurate or even falsified.

Despite any uncertainties, the Barnetts were determined to welcome Natalia into their family. At the time, they were known for their devotion to their children, particularly their prodigious son, Jacob Barnett, a young physics genius. They believed they had the patience and resources to care for a child with special needs.

Initially, everything seemed to be going well. However, as they spent more time with Natalia, doubts began to creep in. Small inconsistencies in her behavior and physical development raised questions about whether she was really the young child they had been led to believe she was. The adoption that was meant to bring joy and fulfillment soon turned into one of the most bewildering and controversial cases in recent history.

Welcoming a New Daughter

When Natalia first arrived at the Barnett household, the family treated her as they would any new child joining a home—offering comfort, affection, and a sense of belonging. Kristine and Michael were initially enthusiastic about their decision, believing they had provided a safe space for a child who had suffered through difficult circumstances.

As a child with a disability, Natalia needed special care. The Barnetts arranged for doctor visits, therapy sessions, and other forms of assistance to help her adjust to her new life in America. They also sought to integrate her into their daily routine, giving her clothes, toys, and a room of her own. Kristine even documented parts of this transition, later using them to highlight how they had treated Natalia as a beloved daughter from the start.

Their three biological sons, particularly Jacob, were also part of this new chapter. Though there were inevitable adjustments, the family appeared welcoming at first. Natalia was included in outings and social gatherings, and they attempted to create a stable home environment for her.

However, as time passed, small inconsistencies in Natalia's behavior became apparent. She showed signs of independence that didn't match what was expected of a six-year-old. She had knowledge and expressions that seemed too mature for a young child. Some of her actions, which might have been dismissed as quirks, began to fuel deeper suspicions.

Despite these early concerns, the Barnetts tried to maintain their commitment to Natalia. They continued to provide for her, hoping that any odd behavior was simply an adjustment period. But as more unsettling incidents occurred, their initial warmth and optimism turned into deep uncertainty. The question of whether they had truly adopted a child—or something far more complicated—began to take hold in their minds.

Early Signs of Doubt and Fear

As the weeks and months passed, the Barnetts' initial excitement about adopting Natalia gave way to confusion, suspicion, and, eventually, fear. The first signs were subtle—things that could have easily been explained away. Natalia's vocabulary and speech patterns seemed more advanced than what was expected of a six-year-old. Her mannerisms at times felt more like those of a teenager or an adult rather than a young child learning to navigate her new home.

Then came the physical evidence. Kristine later stated that she discovered Natalia had already gone through puberty, something that contradicted her reported age. A child of six should not have a menstrual cycle, yet the Barnetts claimed to find evidence that she had one. When she was taken for medical evaluations, doctors gave conflicting opinions—some supported the idea that Natalia was a child, while others suggested she could be much older.

Beyond the medical concerns, Natalia's actions allegedly became disturbing. Kristine and Michael claimed that Natalia made threats against them and their biological children. According to their later accounts, she attempted to harm them in their sleep, made chilling remarks about wanting to kill them, and even displayed violent behavior. The Barnetts described incidents where she tried to push Kristine into an electric fence and poured cleaning chemicals into their coffee.

The combination of these factors—her physical development, her behavior, and the growing fear within the household—made the Barnetts question whether they were truly caring for a helpless child or someone with far darker intentions. This fear would set off a series of events that turned their lives upside down and led to legal battles, media scrutiny, and an international mystery that remains unsolved.

Family Dynamics and Initial Adjustments

Blending a new member into an existing family always presents challenges, but for the Barnetts, bringing Natalia into their home proved to be especially complicated. While they initially tried to embrace her as a daughter, the family's dynamics quickly shifted as doubts about her identity grew.

Kristine, as the primary caregiver, was responsible for overseeing Natalia's daily life. At first, she treated her like any child with special needs, ensuring she received medical care, therapy, and emotional support. However, as questions arose about Natalia's real age and intentions, Kristine's role evolved from mother to investigator. She began scrutinizing Natalia's actions, questioning everything from her ability to care for herself to her understanding of adult topics.

Michael, on the other hand, was initially more passive. In later interviews, he suggested that Kristine was the driving force behind the suspicions. However, as events unfolded, he, too, became concerned about Natalia's behavior and the safety of their children. Their three biological sons were also impacted. Though they were used to being in an intellectually stimulating household—especially given Jacob's status as a child prodigy—living with Natalia introduced new, unfamiliar tensions. Stories later emerged of her making threats or acting aggressively toward them, further straining the family dynamic.

Despite these tensions, the Barnetts tried to make their situation work. They continued to seek medical and psychological opinions to verify Natalia's age and well-being. However, their growing paranoia and the belief that they had been deceived ultimately caused a complete breakdown in trust. Their initial efforts to create a loving family environment had transformed into a household of suspicion and fear, leading them down a path that would change all of their lives forever.

Chapter 2: The Mystery Unfolds

What began as an act of kindness quickly spiraled into a bewildering mystery that gripped both the Barnett family and the public. As time passed, Kristine and Michael Barnett became increasingly convinced that Natalia Grace was not the young child they had believed her to be. Their doubts, initially rooted in inconsistencies in her behavior, were exacerbated by unsettling incidents that seemed far beyond what a six-year-old could be capable of.

Kristine, in particular, became obsessed with uncovering the truth. She began scrutinizing Natalia's past, questioning every detail of her adoption records, medical history, and even her physical development. Her suspicions were amplified by Natalia's interactions with the family—moments of eerie maturity, unexplained knowledge of adult topics, and allegedly violent tendencies.

The mystery deepened when the Barnetts sought medical evaluations. Some doctors suggested that Natalia was much older than her birth certificate indicated, while others maintained she was a child. Conflicting reports only fueled the family's paranoia. Meanwhile, Natalia herself denied all accusations, maintaining that she was just a little girl who wanted a family.

The Barnetts' fears eventually led them to take drastic action: in 2012, they successfully petitioned an Indiana court to legally change Natalia's birth year from 2003 to 1989, making her 22 years old at the time. This shocking move meant that Natalia was no longer considered a minor, allowing the Barnetts to sever legal responsibility for her. Soon after, they moved to Canada with their biological children, leaving Natalia behind in an apartment in Indiana.

The story quickly captured national attention. Was Natalia an innocent orphan wrongly accused, or was she a manipulative adult masquerading as a child? The mystery surrounding her identity and the Barnetts' dramatic claims sparked a media frenzy, but the truth remained elusive.

Questions About Identity and Age

At the heart of this bizarre case is one crucial question: Who is Natalia Grace? Her Ukrainian birth certificate stated she was born in 2003, meaning she would have been six years old at the time of her adoption. However, as time went on, the Barnetts became convinced that this document was either inaccurate or deliberately falsified.

The suspicions arose from a combination of physical, behavioral, and psychological factors. Kristine and Michael pointed to Natalia's adult-like demeanor, advanced vocabulary, and a level of independence that seemed far beyond that of a young child. More concerning, Kristine claimed to have discovered evidence that Natalia had already gone through puberty, something that would be highly unusual for a six-year-old.

The uncertainty surrounding Natalia's true age led to extensive medical examinations, but the results were inconsistent. Some doctors estimated she was a teenager, while others believed she could be in her twenties or even older. One of the most shocking developments came in 2012 when a court ruling, based on select medical opinions and testimonies, legally changed her birth year to 1989, making her an adult in the eyes of the law.

Natalia, however, insisted she was a child. She denied any allegations of deception and claimed she had been abandoned by a family that no longer wanted her. Without definitive proof, the case became a tangled web of conflicting accounts. Was she truly an orphan who had been unfairly accused, or had she manipulated the adoption system to pose as a child and gain entry into a new life in America?

The lack of clear documentation from Ukraine only made matters worse. Without a reliable paper trail, Natalia's true identity remained an enigma—one that legal experts, doctors, and the media struggled to untangle.

Conflicting Medical and Legal Findings

Determining Natalia's real age proved to be one of the most perplexing aspects of the case. Multiple medical evaluations were conducted, yet the results were far from conclusive. Some doctors claimed that based on Natalia's teeth, bone density, and development, she was a child, possibly between eight and ten years old. Others, however, believed she was much older.

One particularly controversial medical opinion came from a doctor who examined Natalia in 2010. He reportedly stated that she was at least 14 years old at the time of adoption. Later evaluations suggested she could be in her late teens or early twenties, pointing to signs of puberty and skeletal development more consistent with an adult. However, other specialists disputed these findings, arguing that dwarfism can affect physical aging markers, making it difficult to determine an exact age.

The legal system only added to the confusion. In 2012, based on select medical opinions, a judge ruled in favor of the Barnetts' petition to change Natalia's birth year from 2003 to 1989. This meant she was legally recognized as an adult, allowing the Barnetts to relinquish their parental obligations.

However, years later, when Natalia found herself in another legal battle, a different medical evaluation contradicted this ruling. A doctor in 2019 testified that Natalia was still a minor, likely around 16 at the time—suggesting that the Barnetts had abandoned a child, not an adult. This contradiction raised serious ethical and legal questions.

Was Natalia's legal age adjustment a mistake? Did the Barnetts manipulate the system to free themselves from responsibility? Or was Natalia actually an adult, successfully deceiving doctors, judges, and the public? With no definitive medical consensus, the case remained mired in uncertainty, leaving both sides armed with their own version of the truth.

Psychological and Behavioral Concerns

Beyond the questions of age and identity, the most disturbing claims in this case revolved around Natalia's behavior. According to the Barnetts, their adopted daughter exhibited deeply unsettling tendencies that made them fear for their safety.

Kristine and Michael alleged that Natalia made threats against them and their biological children. They described incidents where she tried to push Kristine into an electric fence, smeared bodily fluids on walls, and even made comments about wanting to kill them. In the most chilling accusation, they claimed she stood over their beds at night with a knife. These accounts painted the picture of a manipulative and dangerous individual who was pretending to be a child.

However, Natalia and those who supported her offered a very different narrative. She insisted that she never harmed or threatened anyone and that the Barnetts fabricated these stories to justify abandoning her. Some experts suggested that if Natalia did exhibit troubling behavior, it could have stemmed from past trauma, attachment issues, or the stress of transitioning into a new family.

Psychologists who later assessed Natalia offered mixed opinions. Some suggested she showed signs of emotional disturbance, while others believed she was simply a frightened girl who had been misjudged. Dwarfism can sometimes lead to misinterpretations of social cues and behaviors, which may have contributed to the perception of her as manipulative or aggressive.

Regardless of which version of events was true, the psychological aspect of this case added another layer of complexity. Was Natalia a sociopathic adult posing as a child, as the Barnetts claimed? Or was she a vulnerable orphan who had been unfairly villainized? The conflicting accounts made it impossible to determine where the truth really lay, leaving this case one of the most unsettling and debated adoption scandals in modern history.

Chapter 3: A House Divided

The Barnett household, once filled with optimism about welcoming Natalia into their family, soon became a battleground of suspicion, fear, and division. As doubts about Natalia's age and identity grew, so did the fractures within the family dynamic. Kristine and Michael Barnett found themselves at odds, not only with Natalia but also with each other as they debated how to handle the escalating situation.

Kristine was particularly vocal about her belief that Natalia was an adult pretending to be a child. She recounted disturbing incidents that she claimed proved Natalia was a threat. Michael, initially more reserved in his opinions, later supported Kristine's version of events, although some of his statements in court contradicted earlier claims. Their relationship suffered under the weight of the controversy, leading to increased stress, public scrutiny, and eventually, their divorce.

The family's turmoil intensified as they sought medical evaluations and legal interventions to solidify their stance. The court ruling that changed Natalia's birth year from 2003 to 1989 marked a turning point, legally severing the parental bond and further deepening the divide between those who believed Natalia was a helpless child and those convinced she was a dangerous impostor.

Outside the family, friends, neighbors, and even professionals who interacted with Natalia formed their own conflicting opinions. Some saw her as a victim of abandonment, while others sided with the Barnetts. The uncertainty surrounding the case left the family fractured, with no clear path to resolution.

Tensions Between Parents and Their Adopted Child

The relationship between the Barnetts and Natalia rapidly deteriorated as allegations and counterclaims mounted. What began as an adoption intended to provide a loving home quickly turned into a hostile environment filled with mistrust and fear.

Kristine and Michael claimed that Natalia displayed manipulative and even violent behavior soon after joining their family. They alleged that she made threats, engaged in disturbing actions such as smearing bodily fluids on walls, and even attempted to harm them. Kristine described instances where Natalia allegedly tried to poison her, push her into an electric fence, and stood over their beds at night wielding a knife. These claims painted Natalia as a calculating individual capable of extreme deception.

Natalia, on the other hand, vehemently denied these accusations. She maintained that she was just a child struggling to fit into a new home, only to be met with cruelty and rejection. Supporters of Natalia suggested that if she exhibited odd behavior, it was likely due to trauma, attachment issues, or past mistreatment rather than any sinister intent.

The lack of trust between Natalia and the Barnetts ultimately made cohabitation impossible. Kristine and Michael, convinced they were living with an adult imposter, sought legal means to distance themselves from her. The 2012 court ruling legally changing Natalia's age provided the justification they needed to move her into an apartment and cut ties.

Whether Natalia was an abandoned child or a dangerous fraud remained a matter of debate, but the damage to their relationship was irreversible. The conflict between parent and child became one of the most unsettling aspects of the case.

The Impact on Siblings and Extended Family

The tensions between Natalia and the Barnetts did not only affect the parents—it had a profound impact on their biological children and extended family as well. The turmoil within the household created an environment of fear and uncertainty, leaving lasting emotional scars on everyone involved.

The Barnetts' other children, particularly their eldest son Jacob, were directly affected by the chaos. Jacob, a child prodigy with autism, had thrived under his parents' guidance before Natalia's arrival. However, Kristine claimed that Natalia's presence disrupted the family dynamic, making it difficult for Jacob and his siblings to feel safe in their own home. Reports suggest that Natalia's alleged behavior caused distress among the children, though whether she truly posed a danger remains a contested issue.

Extended family members and friends were also drawn into the controversy. Some supported Kristine and Michael, believing their fears were justified, while others questioned the extreme measures they took. The case divided opinions, straining relationships both within and outside the household.

After Natalia was moved into her own apartment, the situation did not improve. The legal battles that followed, along with public scrutiny, placed immense pressure on the Barnett children. As the case gained national attention, they found themselves dragged into a scandal that would follow them for years to come.

For the siblings and extended family, the impact of the controversy was inescapable. Regardless of the truth, the scars left by the ordeal would remain with them long after the media frenzy had faded.

The Struggle to Find the Truth

The case of Natalia Grace became one of the most bewildering and debated adoption scandals in modern history, leaving investigators, medical professionals, and the public struggling to determine the truth. The conflicting claims, shifting narratives, and legal battles made it nearly impossible to establish a definitive account of Natalia's identity.

At the core of the struggle was the question of Natalia's age. The medical evaluations yielded contradictory results—some doctors suggested she was a child, while others believed she was an adult. The legal system further complicated the matter when a judge ruled that she was born in 1989, effectively making her 22 years old at the time. Yet later evaluations challenged this ruling, suggesting she was much younger than legally recognized.

Media outlets sensationalized the case, often presenting extreme viewpoints that either vilified the Barnetts or portrayed Natalia as a con artist. The lack of concrete evidence meant that speculation ran rampant, with the public divided over who was telling the truth.

Meanwhile, Natalia struggled to clear her name, insisting she had never deceived anyone. Those who supported her argued that she had been unjustly abandoned and that the Barnetts' claims were exaggerated to escape parental responsibility. On the other hand, the Barnetts maintained that they had been victims of an elaborate fraud.

To this day, the case remains unresolved in the eyes of many. The struggle to find the truth was hindered by legal loopholes, conflicting medical opinions, and a media circus that only deepened the mystery.

Chapter 4: Legal Battles and Public Scrutiny

As the Natalia Grace case gained national attention, it became entangled in a web of legal battles that left both the Barnetts and Natalia fighting for their reputations. The central issue was whether the Barnetts had legally and ethically severed ties with Natalia, or if they had abandoned a vulnerable child under false pretenses.

In 2012, the Barnetts petitioned the court to change Natalia's birth year from 2003 to 1989, effectively making her an adult in the eyes of the law. This move allowed them to transfer her to an apartment in Lafayette, Indiana, and leave her to live independently. However, when Natalia later claimed she was still a child at the time and had been left alone without proper support, legal questions arose about the Barnetts' responsibilities.

Authorities launched an investigation, leading to charges of neglect against Kristine and Michael Barnett in 2019. Prosecutors argued that if Natalia was indeed a minor, the Barnetts had abandoned a child in need of care. The case became even more complicated when Michael Barnett's testimony appeared to contradict earlier statements, leading to further scrutiny of their motives and actions.

The legal proceedings dragged on, with Natalia providing her own statements in court. Ultimately, the Barnetts were acquitted of neglect charges, but the case left behind lingering doubts and unanswered questions. The legal battles underscored the deep divisions surrounding the case, turning it into one of the most debated adoption scandals in recent history.

The Age Change Controversy

One of the most perplexing aspects of the Natalia Grace case was the controversial decision to legally change her age. The Barnetts successfully petitioned an Indiana court in 2012 to alter her birth year from 2003 to 1989, effectively aging her from 9 to 23 years old overnight. This ruling became a pivotal moment in the case, raising serious ethical and legal questions.

The Barnetts justified the request by presenting medical reports and expert testimonies suggesting Natalia displayed physical and psychological characteristics of an adult. They claimed that dental and bone density tests supported their assertion that she was much older than originally believed. However, other medical evaluations contradicted this, with some doctors stating that she was still a child.

Despite the conflicting opinions, the court sided with the Barnetts, granting the age change without extensive verification. This ruling legally classified Natalia as an adult, stripping her of the protections typically afforded to minors. Critics argue that the decision was rushed and lacked sufficient medical and legal evidence, making it a grave miscarriage of justice if she was indeed a child.

Years later, the controversy over Natalia's true age remains unresolved. The age change ruling created a legal gray area, complicating the case and fueling endless debates. While the Barnetts used the decision to justify their actions, many still question how a legal system could allow such a drastic and life-altering change with so much uncertainty surrounding the truth.

Abandonment Accusations and Courtroom Drama

The Barnetts' decision to leave Natalia in an apartment on her own led to serious allegations of abandonment. In 2019, Indiana prosecutors charged Kristine and Michael Barnett with neglect, claiming they had abandoned a dependent who was unable to care for herself. The legal battle that followed was filled with contradictions, emotional testimonies, and dramatic courtroom moments.

Prosecutors argued that if Natalia was truly a minor, she had been left to fend for herself with no financial or emotional support. They pointed to witness statements from neighbors who recalled Natalia appearing confused and distressed while living alone. Some even claimed she sought help from local families, further suggesting that she was incapable of independent living.

Kristine and Michael, however, maintained that Natalia was an adult and had the capability to live on her own. Michael, who initially supported Kristine's claims, later changed aspects of his testimony, admitting that he had doubts about Natalia's true age. This inconsistency raised questions about whether the Barnetts had manipulated the system to rid themselves of parental responsibility.

In the end, the courts ruled in favor of the Barnetts, dismissing the neglect charges. However, the legal drama left both Natalia and the Barnetts entangled in a narrative full of ambiguity. The trial did not provide a definitive answer about Natalia's age or identity, ensuring that the controversy would persist in public discourse for years to come.

Media Sensationalism and Public Opinion

The Natalia Grace case quickly became a media sensation, drawing comparisons to horror films and real-life con artist stories. Journalists, TV hosts, and internet commentators took sides, fueling speculation and controversy. The media frenzy turned what was already a complex legal battle into a public spectacle, often blurring the lines between fact and sensationalism.

Early reports framed Natalia as a potential fraud, likening her to the plot of *Orphan*, a thriller about a woman posing as a child to infiltrate a family. Headlines painted her as a manipulative adult with sinister intentions, reinforcing the Barnetts' narrative. However, as more details emerged, the story took a different turn, with some outlets questioning the credibility of the Barnetts' claims.

Documentaries and investigative reports sought to unravel the mystery, but instead of providing clear answers, they often fueled more debate. Interviews with Natalia depicted her as a frightened girl who had been wronged, while interviews with the Barnetts portrayed them as desperate parents caught in an impossible situation.

Public opinion was deeply divided. Some people saw Natalia as a dangerous liar who had deceived a well-meaning family, while others believed she was an innocent victim of abandonment and media bias. The rise of social media amplified these debates, with online communities dissecting every piece of evidence, often with little regard for the real-life consequences on those involved.

The relentless media coverage ensured that the case would never truly fade into obscurity. Instead, it became a lasting example of how sensationalism can shape—and sometimes distort—the perception of truth.

Chapter 5: The Fight for Identity

At the core of the Natalia Grace case lies a struggle for identity. Natalia has spent years fighting to prove who she truly is, but her identity remains shrouded in controversy. Was she a vulnerable child abandoned by the very people who promised her a loving home, or was she an adult fraudulently posing as a child to exploit a family's generosity?

After being adopted from Ukraine, Natalia was initially recognized as a young girl. However, when the Barnetts petitioned to have her age legally changed to 22, she was suddenly thrust into adulthood—at least in the eyes of the law. This decision drastically altered the course of her life, stripping her of the protections and opportunities afforded to minors.

For Natalia, the battle to reclaim her identity is not just about legal records but about the very foundation of who she is. Despite multiple medical opinions, court rulings, and public scrutiny, a definitive answer about her real age has never been reached.

Her story is one of displacement and uncertainty. Without clear documentation of her past, Natalia has had to navigate a world where many people doubt her claims. The legal and social conflicts surrounding her case have made it nearly impossible for her to move forward with a stable sense of self.

Her fight for identity remains ongoing, as she continues to challenge the narrative that has defined her life, seeking recognition not just in the courtroom but in the court of public opinion.

Natalia's Side of the Story

While much of the media attention initially focused on the Barnetts' version of events, Natalia has worked to share her own perspective. In interviews and legal statements, she has adamantly denied ever deceiving the Barnetts or pretending to be older than she actually was. Instead, she claims she was an innocent child abandoned under shocking circumstances.

According to Natalia, she was blindsided when her adoptive parents began accusing her of being an adult. She recalls being treated as a daughter at first, but as the months passed, she noticed a change in their behavior. Kristine Barnett, in particular, allegedly became more suspicious, scrutinizing Natalia's actions and questioning her age.

Natalia insists she was never violent or manipulative, as the Barnetts claimed. Instead, she describes feeling increasingly isolated and frightened as her adoptive family distanced themselves from her. She maintains that she never had the knowledge or life experience of an adult and struggled greatly when left alone in an apartment with no support.

Her story is backed by medical professionals who examined her and testified that she was still a child when the Barnetts abandoned her. Despite this, Natalia's age remains a point of contention, leaving her trapped in a legal limbo.

By speaking out, Natalia hopes to reclaim her voice and shed light on the suffering she endured. Yet, with the case so deeply polarizing, she continues to face skepticism and public scrutiny, making her fight for justice even more difficult.

A Life Caught Between Two Realities

Natalia Grace's life has been defined by two competing narratives—one that casts her as a cunning imposter and another that sees her as an abandoned child. The conflict between these perspectives has left her in a painful and confusing existence, struggling to prove her truth while the world debates her identity.

On one hand, the legal system recognizes her as an adult, thanks to the court ruling that changed her age. This decision has denied her the resources and support that a minor would typically receive. She has been forced to fend for herself, despite her claims that she was too young to do so when first left alone.

On the other hand, Natalia's own experiences and the testimonies of some medical experts suggest that she was indeed a child at the time of her adoption. If true, she was placed in an unimaginable situation—forced into adulthood against her will, unable to access education, legal protections, or a family to guide her.

This dual reality has made it nearly impossible for Natalia to establish a stable life. Without definitive proof of her real age, she exists in a strange in-between state—legally an adult but potentially still a child when her abandonment took place.

Her case highlights the devastating consequences of bureaucratic and legal failures, where a person can be trapped in circumstances beyond their control. Until the truth is fully established, Natalia will continue living in the shadow of uncertainty, caught between two conflicting identities.

The Emotional and Psychological Toll

The uncertainty surrounding Natalia Grace's identity has taken a significant emotional and psychological toll on her. From the moment her age was questioned, she has endured relentless scrutiny, abandonment, and public speculation, all of which have shaped her mental and emotional well-being.

Being accused of deception by the people who were supposed to protect her left deep scars.

Natalia has spoken about the pain of feeling unwanted and discarded, as the Barnetts not only abandoned her but also framed her as a dangerous fraud. The isolation of being left alone at such a young age—without guidance or security—would have been overwhelming for anyone, let alone someone who believed they were a child.

Additionally, the constant media coverage and public debate about her identity have only added to her distress. Every aspect of her life has been dissected, with strangers forming opinions about her based on incomplete or conflicting information. Living under such intense scrutiny has made it difficult for Natalia to move forward, as the controversy continues to follow her.

Even after the legal battles, Natalia is still dealing with the emotional impact of her experiences. The trauma of abandonment, coupled with the struggle to be believed, has created lasting psychological challenges. While she has tried to rebuild her life, the weight of her past continues to haunt her, serving as a reminder of the family she lost and the identity she has yet to fully reclaim.

Chapter 6: The Fallout and Where They Are Now

The Natalia Grace case captured global attention, but as the media frenzy faded, the individuals involved were left to deal with the consequences of years of legal battles, public scrutiny, and personal turmoil. The fallout from the case affected not only Natalia but also her adoptive parents, the Barnetts, and everyone connected to the controversy.

For Natalia, the fight to prove her identity and rebuild her life has been an ongoing struggle. She remains a highly publicized figure, with her story continuing to spark debates about adoption, legal loopholes, and child welfare. Despite gaining some support, she still faces skepticism from those who believe the Barnetts' version of events.

Meanwhile, Michael and Kristine Barnett, once seen as model parents, have had their lives irrevocably altered. Their claims against Natalia led to legal charges and intense media scrutiny, which impacted their reputations and personal lives. The couple's divorce and their legal battles have only added to the complexity of their situation.

Other key players in the case, including medical professionals, legal authorities, and social workers, have also faced public and professional challenges as a result of their involvement. Some have stood by their assessments, while others have distanced themselves from the controversy.

The case remains a cautionary tale about the dangers of rushed legal decisions, the power of media narratives, and the long-lasting effects of uncertainty in adoption cases. Even years later, the truth remains elusive, and the fallout continues to shape the lives of those involved.

The Fate of the Adoptive Parents

Michael and Kristine Barnett went from being celebrated as devoted parents to being at the center of a shocking and complex legal battle. Once praised for raising a prodigious son, they became infamous for abandoning Natalia and accusing her of being an adult con artist. The accusations they made against Natalia led to criminal charges, extensive media coverage, and a public reckoning that dramatically altered their lives.

The legal proceedings against the Barnetts were lengthy and controversial. They were charged with neglect after allegedly abandoning Natalia in an apartment and moving to Canada. Michael and Kristine, however, maintained that they were the true victims, claiming they had been deceived into adopting an adult who posed a threat to their family.

Eventually, Michael was acquitted of all charges in 2022, and the case against Kristine was dismissed. Despite this, their reputations suffered greatly, and their personal lives became deeply strained. The couple divorced, and their once-close-knit family dynamic shattered under the weight of the controversy.

Kristine, who had been an advocate for children with special needs, largely disappeared from public life, while Michael continued to defend his actions in interviews and legal proceedings. Regardless of their legal outcomes, the Barnetts remain figures of controversy, with some believing their claims and others condemning them for abandoning a vulnerable child.

The fate of the Barnetts serves as a stark reminder of how a single adoption case unraveled into a life-altering crisis, leaving behind a trail of unanswered questions and irreversible damage.

Natalia's Journey Toward Independence

After years of being at the center of a media firestorm, Natalia Grace has had to forge a path toward independence while carrying the weight of her past. Her journey has not been easy, as she has had to navigate life with lingering doubts about her identity, limited support, and a world that continues to scrutinize her every move.

Since her abandonment, Natalia has worked to establish stability in her life. She has received assistance from new guardians and individuals who believe in her story, helping her transition into adulthood—whether she was truly a child at the time or not. She has also spoken out about her experiences, sharing her side of the story in interviews and documentaries to shed light on what she endured.

Despite her efforts, rebuilding her life has come with challenges. The stigma surrounding her case makes it difficult for her to move forward without facing judgment or speculation. Finding work, building relationships, and even maintaining a sense of normalcy have been complicated by the notoriety of her past.

However, Natalia remains determined to create a future for herself, separate from the controversy that defined her early years in the United States. Whether through education, advocacy, or simply reclaiming her personal identity, she continues to push forward, seeking stability and self-sufficiency in a world that still debates the truth about her past.

Conclusion

The Natalia Grace case remains one of the most perplexing and controversial adoption stories in recent history. What began as an opportunity for a young girl to find a loving home spiraled into a legal, medical, and media spectacle that left the world questioning the very nature of truth, identity, and justice. Years later, the case continues to spark debates about adoption ethics, the legal system's handling of age disputes, and the influence of media sensationalism on public perception.

For Natalia, the battle for her identity and stability has been long and challenging. Whether seen as a victim or a manipulator, she has had to navigate the fallout of accusations that have followed her into adulthood. Meanwhile, the Barnetts, once celebrated as dedicated parents, have endured public scrutiny, legal battles, and personal upheaval, all while standing by their claims that they were deceived.

The case serves as a cautionary tale about the dangers of rushed legal decisions, the complexities of adoption, and the power of media narratives in shaping public opinion. While some questions have been answered, many remain unresolved, leaving room for speculation, doubt, and ongoing curiosity.

In the end, the Natalia Grace saga is a reminder that truth is often more complex than it appears. As those involved attempt to move forward, their stories continue to serve as a testament to the profound and lasting consequences of a mystery that may never be fully unraveled.

www.ingramcontent.com/pod-product-compliance
Ingram Content Group UK Ltd.
Pitfield, Milton Keynes, MK11 3LW, UK
UKHW021508150425
5491UKWH00030B/513